The Comprehensive Blockchain Technology Career Guide

Decentralizing Your Potential

Michael McNaught

Considering a career in the Technology Industry? Have you ever considered Blockchain Technology careers? Well… look no further, this guide is for you! Blockchain Technology is rapidly becoming more popular and even more lucrative.

Copyright

The Comprehensive Blockchain Technology Career Guide: Decentralizing Your Potential

Written By Michael McNaught

Table of Contents

Preface

Hi there! My name is Michael McNaught, a Scientist by profession, and an avid Blockchain and crypto enthusiast. I enjoy learning about cutting-edge technology and sharing my knowledge with others.

Welcome to the forefront of innovation! Welcome to the blockchain revolution. This guidebook is a roadmap, a compass, and a companion for anyone curious about or committed to forging a career in the transformative realm of blockchain technology.

In these pages, my aim is to demystify the complexities and illuminate the pathways that lead to thriving careers within this dynamic landscape. From the foundational principles of blockchain to the myriad roles, skills, and opportunities that abound, this book serves as a concise yet comprehensive introduction to the world of blockchain careers.

Whether you're an aspiring developer seeking to harness the power of smart contracts or a professional intrigued by the decentralized potential of blockchain across industries, this guidebook endeavors to equip you with insights, practical advice, and a panoramic view of the possibilities that await.

Embracing blockchain isn't just about mastering coding languages or understanding cryptographic protocols—it's about embracing a mindset of innovation, adaptability, and continuous learning. I invite you to explore the diverse paths, engage with the community, and chart your course towards a rewarding career in this ever-evolving domain.

As the pages turn, consider this book not just as a resource, but as a catalyst for your journey, one that invites you to embark on an adventure where disruption meets opportunity, and where the future is being shaped one block at a time.

Chapter 1: Foundations of Blockchain

-What is Blockchain?

Blockchain is a decentralized, distributed ledger technology that records transactions across a network of computers in a way that is secure, transparent, and immutable. Here's a breakdown:

> Decentralization: Traditional databases are often centralized, meaning one entity (like a company or government) controls the data. In contrast, a blockchain is decentralized, spread across a network of computers (nodes). Each node has a copy of the entire blockchain, ensuring no single authority has control.

> Blocks and Chains: Transactions are grouped into blocks, each containing a list of transactions and a reference to the previous block. These blocks are cryptographically linked in a sequential chain, forming the blockchain. Once a block is added, it's challenging to alter previous blocks, ensuring data integrity.

> Consensus Mechanisms: To validate and add new blocks to the chain, a consensus mechanism is used. Various mechanisms exist (like Proof of Work, Proof of Stake, etc.), each with its way of ensuring agreement among nodes regarding the validity of transactions.

> Immutability and Security: Once a block is added to the chain, it's extremely difficult to alter it due to the cryptographic hash functions linking blocks.

Changing one block would require changing subsequent blocks on all copies of the ledger across the network. Doing this is computationally infeasible. This security feature maintains the integrity of the data.

Transparency: Blockchain transactions are transparent and visible to all participants in the network. While the data is transparent, the identities of the participants might be pseudonymous, depending on the type of blockchain.

Smart Contracts: These are self-executing contracts with the terms directly written into code. They automatically enforce and execute agreed-upon actions when predefined conditions are met. Smart contracts run on the blockchain, providing efficiency, security, and automation of various processes.

Use Cases: Blockchain technology gained attention initially as the underlying technology for cryptocurrencies like Bitcoin and Ethereum. However, its applications go beyond finance, encompassing supply chain management, healthcare, voting systems, identity verification, and more. It's valued for its ability to enhance transparency, security, and efficiency in various sectors.

In summary, blockchain is a groundbreaking technology offering a secure, transparent, and decentralized way to record and verify transactions and other data across a network. Its potential to revolutionize various industries lies in its ability to provide trust in a trustless environment without the need for intermediaries.

-How Does Blockchain Work?

Blockchain works through a combination of decentralized consensus, cryptographic principles, and a network of nodes. Here's a step-by-step breakdown of how it operates:

Transactions: Participants initiate transactions. These could involve the transfer of cryptocurrency, recording ownership, executing smart contracts, or any data interaction that needs validation.

Block Formation: Transactions are grouped into blocks. Each block contains a list of these transactions and a reference (hash) to the previous block in the chain.

Validation and Consensus: Nodes on the network validate the transactions in the block. Various consensus mechanisms (like Proof of Work, Proof of Stake, etc.) are employed to ensure agreement among nodes about the validity of the transactions.

Adding the Block: Once validated, the new block is added to the existing blockchain. The chain continues to grow, with each new block containing a reference to the previous one, creating an unbroken sequence.

Decentralization: Copies of the entire blockchain exist on each node in the network. This decentralization ensures no single entity controls the data and that all nodes have an identical copy of the ledger.

Security through Cryptography: Each block is linked to the previous one through cryptographic hashes. Changing any block would require recalculating subsequent blocks' hashes across the network, making tampering extremely difficult and preserving the integrity of the data.

Consensus Maintenance: The consensus mechanism continues to operate, ensuring that all nodes on the network agree on the state of the blockchain, thereby maintaining its integrity and consistency.

Immutability: Once a block is added to the blockchain, it becomes extremely challenging to alter any information within it. This immutability ensures that historical data remains secure and unchangeable.

Transparency: While the data within the blockchain is transparent and visible to participants, the level of anonymity or pseudonymity can vary based on the blockchain's design.

Smart Contracts (Optional): Some blockchains support smart contracts, enabling self-executing contracts with predefined conditions written into code. These contracts automatically execute actions when conditions are met, running on the blockchain without the need for intermediaries.

In summary, blockchain operates as a decentralized, secure, and transparent ledger system. It relies on consensus among nodes, cryptographic principles, and an unbroken chain of blocks to ensure the integrity, security, and transparency of recorded transactions and data across a network.

-Types of Blockchains

There are primarily three types of blockchains based on their accessibility and permissions:

Public Blockchains: These are open and permissionless networks where anyone can participate, view, and contribute to the blockchain. Bitcoin and Ethereum are notable examples. Public blockchains are decentralized and offer high transparency and security but might have scalability issues and higher energy consumption.

Private Blockchains: These are permissioned networks where only authorized participants can access and participate in the blockchain. Access control is managed by an entity, making them more centralized than public blockchains. Private blockchains are often used by enterprises and businesses for internal operations, providing more privacy, scalability, and efficiency but sacrificing decentralization.

Consortium (Federated) Blockchains: These are semi-decentralized networks where a limited number of nodes control the consensus process. Consortium blockchains are typically used by a group of organizations that work together, sharing authority over the network. They offer a balance between the openness of public blockchains and the control of private blockchains, providing controlled access, scalability, and privacy among a defined set of participants.

Additionally, blockchains can be categorized based on their consensus mechanisms:

Proof of Work (PoW): This consensus mechanism, used by Bitcoin, requires miners to solve complex mathematical puzzles to validate transactions and create new blocks. It's energy-intensive but highly secure.

Proof of Stake (PoS): In PoS, validators are chosen to create new blocks based on the number of coins they hold and are willing to "stake" as collateral. PoS is more energy-efficient than PoW and has different variations like Delegated Proof of Stake (DPoS) and Proof of Authority (PoA). The Ethereum blockchain uses the PoS system.

Other Consensus Mechanisms: There are various other consensus mechanisms like Proof of Burn, Proof of Space, and more, each with its way of achieving agreement among nodes while addressing issues like scalability, energy consumption, and security.

These different types and classifications cater to various needs, offering a spectrum of trade-offs between decentralization, scalability, privacy, and control, making blockchain technology adaptable to diverse use cases and industries.

-Smart Contracts and Decentralized Applications (DApps)

Smart contracts and decentralized applications (DApps) are integral components of blockchain technology:

Smart Contracts:

Definition: Smart contracts are self-executing contracts with the terms of the agreement directly written into code. They automatically enforce and execute actions or agreements when predefined conditions are met.

Functionality: Smart contracts operate on a blockchain, allowing for trustless and automated execution of various processes without intermediaries. They execute actions based on the predetermined rules encoded in the contract.

Features: These contracts can facilitate the exchange of money, property, shares, or anything of value transparently, securely, and without the need for middlemen. Once deployed, they run exactly as programmed, ensuring precise and tamper-proof execution.

Use Cases: Smart contracts find applications in various fields such as finance, supply chain management, real estate, voting systems, and more. For instance, in finance, they can automate loan agreements or execute trades without the need for brokers.

Decentralized Applications (DApps):

Definition: DApps are applications built on a decentralized network (usually a blockchain) with no central point of control. They use smart contracts as their backend logic to enable decentralized functionality.

Characteristics: DApps aim to be open-source, transparent, and often operate with tokens or cryptocurrencies. They are designed to run on a peer-to-peer network rather than a centralized server, ensuring greater security and reliability.

Types: DApps can be categorized into various types based on their functionalities, such as financial DApps (DeFi - Decentralized Finance), gaming DApps, social media platforms, supply chain management solutions, etc.

Advantages: DApps offer increased security, data integrity, transparency, and censorship resistance. They provide users with more control over their data and interactions, eliminating reliance on central authorities.

Challenges: Developing DApps often involves overcoming scalability issues, user adoption challenges, and ensuring a smooth user experience while maintaining the principles of decentralization.

In essence, smart contracts enable automated and trustless execution of agreements or actions, while DApps leverage these smart contracts as their backend to create decentralized applications that operate on a peer-to-peer network, promoting transparency, security, and user empowerment.

Chapter 2: Industries Disrupted by Blockchain

Blockchain has disrupted various industries by introducing several transformative elements:

Finance and Banking:

> *Payments and Transactions:* Blockchain technology has revolutionized payments and remittances by enabling faster, cheaper, and more transparent cross-border transactions. Cryptocurrencies like Bitcoin and stablecoins facilitate these transactions without the need for intermediaries.

> *Smart Contracts:* Financial institutions use smart contracts for automated loan agreements, insurance claims processing, and executing complex financial contracts without manual intervention, reducing costs and enhancing efficiency.

Supply Chain and Logistics:

> *Traceability and Transparency:* Blockchain enhances supply chain transparency by enabling the tracking of products from origin to destination. It ensures authenticity, reduces fraud, and allows consumers to verify the origin and history of products, especially in industries like food, pharmaceuticals, and luxury goods.

> *Efficiency in Operations:* Smart contracts automate and streamline supply chain processes, facilitating faster and more accurate transactions between stakeholders.

Healthcare:

Data Security and Interoperability: Blockchain secures patient data by providing a tamper-proof and decentralized way of storing medical records. It enables secure sharing of patient data among healthcare providers, improving interoperability while maintaining data privacy.

Drug Traceability: Blockchain helps track the authenticity and movement of pharmaceuticals, reducing the circulation of counterfeit drugs and ensuring compliance with regulations.

Real Estate:

Property Transactions: Blockchain facilitates faster and more transparent real estate transactions by providing a secure and immutable record of property ownership and transfer. Smart contracts streamline processes like property sales, rental agreements, and title transfers, reducing paperwork and fraud.

Entertainment and Gaming:

Digital Ownership: Blockchain enables ownership of digital assets, such as in-game items, artwork, music, and videos. Players can have true ownership and trade these assets securely on blockchain-based platforms.

Transparent Royalty Payments: Musicians and artists can receive fair and transparent royalty payments through blockchain, ensuring that they get compensated directly and fairly for their work.

Others:

Voting Systems: Blockchain offers secure and transparent voting systems, minimizing fraud and ensuring the integrity of elections by providing an immutable record of votes.

Identity Verification: Blockchain-based identity verification systems enhance security and privacy by allowing individuals to control and manage their digital identities securely.

In each of these industries, blockchain technology introduces efficiency, transparency, security, and reduced dependency on intermediaries, leading to significant disruptions and transformations in traditional processes.

Chapter 3: Career Paths in Blockchain Technology

Here's an overview of career paths in blockchain technology along with examples of each role:

1. Blockchain Developer:

Role: Blockchain developers specialize in building decentralized applications (DApps) and smart contracts on blockchain platforms. They write code, design protocols, and ensure the functionality and security of blockchain-based systems.

Example: A blockchain developer might work on creating a decentralized finance (DeFi) application using Ethereum smart contracts to facilitate lending and borrowing without intermediaries.

-Blockchain Developer salary, available jobs and career outlook

As of 2022, the career outlook for Blockchain Developers was robust, with growing demand for skilled professionals in various industries. However, keep in mind that the job market and salaries can vary based on factors like location, experience, and specific skill sets. Here's a general overview:

Salary:

In the United States, Blockchain Developers' salaries typically ranged from $150,000 to $175,000 per year (dappuniversity.com), depending on factors like experience, expertise, and location. Senior developers or those with specialized skills could earn even more.

Available Jobs:

Job opportunities for Blockchain Developers were increasing across sectors like finance, supply chain, healthcare, and technology.

Positions included Blockchain Developers, Smart Contract Developers, Solidity Developers, Blockchain Engineers, and more.

Startups, tech companies, financial institutions, and consulting firms were among the entities actively hiring for blockchain-related roles.

Career Outlook:

The demand for Blockchain Developers was expected to grow as more industries explored and adopted blockchain technology.

Skills in blockchain development, smart contract writing, and familiarity with various blockchain platforms (Ethereum, Hyperledger, etc.) were highly sought after.

Continuous learning and staying updated with the evolving blockchain ecosystem were essential to maintain competitiveness in the job market.

For the most current and location-specific information regarding salaries, job availability, and career outlook in the field of blockchain development, I would recommend checking recent job listings, industry reports, and salary surveys specific to your region or country. Additionally, networking within blockchain communities and staying informed about industry trends and advancements will provide valuable insights into the current job market and career prospects.

2. **Blockchain Engineer:**

Role: Blockchain engineers focus on the architecture and infrastructure of blockchain networks. They design and implement protocols, optimize network performance, and handle scalability issues.

Example: A blockchain engineer could be responsible for designing consensus mechanisms for a permissioned blockchain network in a supply chain management system.

-Blockchain Engineer salary, available jobs and career outlook

As of 2022, the demand for Blockchain Engineers was rising due to the increasing adoption of blockchain technology across industries. Here's an overview of the salary, job availability, and career outlook:

Salary:

The salary range for Blockchain Engineers varied significantly based on factors like location, experience, and specific skills. In the United States, salaries typically ranged from $63,000 to $205,000 annually (ziprecuiter.com). Senior-level positions or those with specialized expertise could command higher salaries.

Available Jobs:

Job opportunities for Blockchain Engineers were expanding across sectors including finance, supply chain, healthcare, and tech companies.

Positions included Blockchain Engineer, Blockchain Architect, Consensus Algorithm Engineer, Blockchain Infrastructure Engineer, and more.

Both established companies and startups were actively recruiting Blockchain Engineers to develop and implement blockchain solutions.

Career Outlook:

The career outlook for Blockchain Engineers remained positive, with a growing number of companies investing in blockchain projects.

The demand was particularly strong for individuals with expertise in blockchain protocols (like Ethereum, Hyperledger), smart contract development, consensus algorithms, and expertise in cryptography.

Continuous learning and staying updated with emerging blockchain technologies and their real-world applications were essential for career advancement.

It's important to note that the job market and salaries in the blockchain field can evolve rapidly. Factors such as new technological advancements, regulatory changes, and market demand can influence career opportunities and salary ranges.

For the most current and location-specific information regarding salaries, job availability, and the career outlook in the field of Blockchain Engineering, I recommend checking recent job listings, industry reports, and salary surveys specific to your region or country. Additionally, networking within blockchain communities and staying informed about industry trends will provide valuable insights into the current job market and career prospects.

3. **Cryptocurrency Analyst:**

> Role: Cryptocurrency analysts study market trends, analyze digital asset performance, and provide insights to investors or businesses. They track market movements, assess risk factors, and forecast cryptocurrency values.

> Example: A cryptocurrency analyst might analyze Bitcoin's price fluctuations and market sentiment to provide investment recommendations to clients or management.

-Cryptocurrency Analyst salary, available jobs and career outlook

As of 2022, the field of cryptocurrency analysis was experiencing growth and increasing demand due to the expanding cryptocurrency market. Here's an overview of the salary, job availability, and career outlook for Cryptocurrency Analysts:

Salary:

Cryptocurrency Analyst salaries varied based on factors like location, experience, and the specific role within the field. In the United States, salaries for Cryptocurrency Analysts typically ranged from $33,000 to $120,000 annually (ziprecuiter.com).

Senior-level positions, those with extensive experience, or working for high-profile financial firms might command higher salaries.

Available Jobs:

Job opportunities for Cryptocurrency Analysts were expanding across various sectors, including finance, investment firms, crypto exchanges, hedge funds, and research organizations.

Positions included Cryptocurrency Analyst, Crypto Market Analyst, Investment Analyst (focused on digital assets), Crypto Researcher, and more.

Both established financial institutions and startups in the cryptocurrency space were hiring analysts to provide insights into market trends, investment strategies, and risk assessment related to digital assets.

Career Outlook:

The career outlook for Cryptocurrency Analysts remained positive, with the growing importance of cryptocurrencies in the financial sector.

Strong analytical skills, a deep understanding of market trends, knowledge of blockchain technology, and the ability to analyze data related to cryptocurrencies were highly valued in the industry.

Continuous learning, staying updated with market trends, regulatory changes, and advancements in the cryptocurrency space were essential for career growth and remaining competitive.

Please note that the cryptocurrency market is highly dynamic and can experience rapid changes in job demand, salary ranges, and industry developments. The job market might have evolved since the printing of this book, therefore, I recommend checking recent job listings, industry reports, and salary surveys specific to your region or country for the most current information on job availability and salary trends for Cryptocurrency Analysts. Networking within the cryptocurrency and finance communities can also provide valuable insights into the current job market and career prospects.

4. Blockchain Project Manager:

Role: Blockchain project managers oversee blockchain-related projects, coordinate teams, set project timelines, and ensure successful delivery. They bridge the gap between technical teams and stakeholders.

Example: A blockchain project manager could lead the implementation of a blockchain-based supply chain solution for a multinational company, ensuring smooth execution and meeting business objectives.

-Blockchain Project Manager Analyst salary, available jobs and career outlook

As of 2022, Blockchain Project Managers and Analysts were in demand as companies increasingly explored and implemented blockchain solutions. Here's an overview of their salary, job availability, and career outlook:

Salary:

Salaries for Blockchain Project Managers and Analysts varied based on factors such as location, experience, and the industry in which they worked. In the United States, salaries typically ranged from $28,000 to $113,000 annually (ziprecuiter.com).

Senior-level positions, extensive experience in project management, and specialized expertise in blockchain projects could command higher salaries.

Available Jobs:

Job opportunities for Blockchain Project Managers and Analysts were increasing across various sectors, including finance, supply chain, healthcare, and technology companies.

Positions included Blockchain Project Manager, Blockchain Business Analyst, Blockchain Implementation Analyst, and more.

Both established companies and startups exploring blockchain technology were seeking professionals to oversee, plan, and execute blockchain projects, ensuring successful integration and alignment with business objectives.

Career Outlook:

The career outlook for Blockchain Project Managers and Analysts was promising, reflecting the growing adoption of blockchain solutions across industries.

Professionals with a blend of project management expertise and a deep understanding of blockchain technology were highly sought after.

Strong communication skills, the ability to bridge technical and non-technical teams, and a strategic approach to implementing blockchain solutions were essential for success in these roles.

The job market and salary ranges in the blockchain industry can evolve rapidly. Factors such as new technological advancements, industry adoption rates, and market demand for blockchain-based solutions can influence career opportunities and salary trends.

For the most current and location-specific information regarding salaries, job availability, and the career outlook in the field of Blockchain Project Management and Analysis,

I recommend checking recent job listings, industry reports, and salary surveys specific to your region or country. Networking within blockchain communities and staying informed about industry trends will provide valuable insights into the current job market and career prospects.

5. Blockchain UX/UI Designer:

Role: UX/UI designers in blockchain focus on creating user-friendly interfaces for blockchain applications. They ensure that DApps are intuitive, visually appealing, and easy to navigate.

Example: A blockchain UX/UI designer might work on designing an intuitive interface for a decentralized exchange (DEX) platform, making trading and token swaps seamless for users.

-Blockchain UX/UI Designer salary, available jobs and career outlook

As of 2022, the field of Blockchain UX/UI Design was gaining prominence as blockchain applications expanded. Here's an overview of the salary, job availability, and career outlook for Blockchain UX/UI Designers:

Salary:

Salaries for Blockchain UX/UI Designers varied based on factors like location, experience, and the specific role within the field. In the United States, salaries typically ranged from $70,000 to $150,000 annually (linkedin.com).

Senior-level positions, those with extensive experience in UX/UI design and specialization in blockchain-related projects, could command higher salaries.

Available Jobs:

Job opportunities for Blockchain UX/UI Designers were growing, especially in companies developing decentralized applications (DApps), blockchain platforms, or crypto wallets.

Positions included Blockchain UX/UI Designer, DApp Designer, Crypto Wallet Designer, and more.

Both established blockchain companies and startups in the crypto space were seeking designers capable of creating user-friendly interfaces for blockchain-based applications.

Career Outlook:

The career outlook for Blockchain UX/UI Designers appeared promising, considering the increasing demand for well-designed and user-friendly blockchain applications.

Professionals with a strong background in UX/UI design, a deep understanding of blockchain principles, and the ability to create intuitive interfaces for decentralized applications were highly valued.

Being adaptable to the unique requirements and constraints of blockchain interfaces, as well as staying updated with the evolving blockchain ecosystem, were crucial for career growth in this field.

Please note that the job market and salaries in the blockchain industry can evolve rapidly. Factors such as technological advancements, the emergence of new blockchain platforms, and changes in user preferences can impact job availability and salary ranges.

For the most current and location-specific information regarding salaries, job availability, and the career outlook in the field of Blockchain UX/UI Design, as always, I recommend checking recent job listings, industry reports, and salary surveys specific to your region or country. Networking within blockchain and design communities can also provide valuable insights into the current job market and career prospects.

6. **Legal and Regulatory Experts in Blockchain:**

Role: Legal and regulatory experts in blockchain specialize in navigating the complex legal landscape surrounding cryptocurrencies, smart contracts, and blockchain technology. They ensure compliance with regulations and advise on legal implications.

Example: A legal expert might provide counsel to a blockchain startup regarding regulatory compliance for launching an Initial Coin Offering (ICO) or navigating data privacy laws.

-Legal and Regulatory Experts in Blockchain salary, available jobs and career outlook

As of 2022, the demand for Legal and Regulatory Experts in Blockchain was on the rise as the blockchain industry encountered complex legal landscapes and regulatory frameworks. Here's an overview of the salary, job availability, and career outlook for these professionals:

Salary:

> Salaries for Legal and Regulatory Experts in Blockchain varied widely based on factors like location, experience, and the specific role or organization. In the United States, salaries typically ranged from $45,000 to $138,000 annually (ziprecuiter.com).

> Senior-level positions, extensive experience in legal and regulatory matters related to blockchain, or roles in high-profile firms might command higher salaries.

Available Jobs:

> Job opportunities for Legal and Regulatory Experts in Blockchain were growing across various sectors, including finance, technology, legal firms specializing in blockchain, and regulatory compliance entities.

> Positions included Blockchain Legal Counsel, Regulatory Compliance Analyst, Blockchain Policy Advisor, and more.

> Companies dealing with cryptocurrencies, blockchain platforms, exchanges, and fintech

startups were seeking legal professionals capable of navigating the complex regulatory landscape.

Career Outlook:

The career outlook for Legal and Regulatory Experts in Blockchain appeared promising, given the evolving nature of blockchain technology and the need for expertise in compliance and legal matters.

Professionals with a strong understanding of blockchain technology, expertise in regulatory compliance, and the ability to interpret and navigate the legal implications of blockchain initiatives were highly valued.

Staying updated with changing regulations, international compliance standards, and actively engaging with policymakers and industry bodies were essential for career growth in this field.

Please note that the job market and salaries in the blockchain industry can evolve rapidly. Factors such as regulatory changes, government policies, and the maturation of the blockchain ecosystem can impact job availability and salary ranges.

For the most current and location-specific information regarding salaries, job availability, and the career outlook in the field of Legal and Regulatory Experts in Blockchain, I recommend checking recent job listings, industry reports, and salary surveys specific to your region or country. Networking within legal, regulatory, and blockchain communities can also provide valuable insights into the current job market and career prospects.

7. Entrepreneurship and Startups in Blockchain:

Role: Entrepreneurs in blockchain identify innovative opportunities, create startups, and develop new business models using blockchain technology. They might focus on launching new DApps, creating token economies, or offering blockchain-based services.

Example: An entrepreneur could establish a startup aiming to revolutionize the music industry by creating a decentralized platform for artists to directly connect with fans and manage royalties using smart contracts.

These career paths illustrate the diverse opportunities within the blockchain space, catering to technical, managerial, creative, legal, and entrepreneurial skill sets, all contributing to the growth and innovation within the industry.

-Entrepreneurship and Startups in Blockchain salary, available jobs and career outlook

For individuals pursuing entrepreneurship and startups in the blockchain space, assessing salary or conventional job availability might not align with the typical corporate roles. However, understanding the potential for growth, opportunities, and the overall career outlook in this sector is crucial. Here's an overview:

Salary:

In the realm of entrepreneurship and startups, compensation structures are often tied to the success and growth of the venture rather than a fixed salary. Founders and entrepreneurs typically earn income through equity, funding rounds, or dividends once the business gains traction.

The potential for financial rewards in successful blockchain startups can be substantial, but it's also associated with high risk and uncertainty, especially in the early stages.

Available Opportunities:

Opportunities in blockchain entrepreneurship involve identifying innovative ideas, building decentralized applications (DApps), creating new blockchain-based solutions, or establishing platforms that leverage blockchain technology.

Startup roles might include founders, co-founders, developers, product managers, marketing experts, and other team members crucial to the success of a blockchain startup.

Career Outlook:

The career outlook in blockchain entrepreneurship is driven by the rapid evolution of technology, the continuous discovery of new use cases, and the disruptive potential of blockchain across industries.

Entrepreneurs in this space have the opportunity to pioneer groundbreaking solutions, disrupt traditional sectors, and potentially influence the future of technology and finance.

Success in blockchain entrepreneurship relies on a combination of innovation, business acumen, technical expertise, adaptability to market changes, and the ability to navigate regulatory landscapes.

While salaries and conventional job availability might not directly apply to entrepreneurship in blockchain, the potential for growth and impact within this innovative space is significant. Success in blockchain entrepreneurship involves a blend of vision, perseverance, and seizing opportunities in an industry that continues to redefine how businesses operate and interact globally.

Chapter 4: Building Skills for a Career in Blockchain

Here's a breakdown of required skills for a successful career in blockchain:

1. Programming Languages for Blockchain Development:

> Solidity: Solidity is a primary programming language for creating smart contracts on Ethereum. Learning Solidity is crucial for developing decentralized applications (DApps) and executing automated contracts.

> Other Languages: Proficiency in languages like JavaScript, Python, or C++ is beneficial as they are used in blockchain development beyond smart contracts.

2. Understanding Solidity and Smart Contract Development:

> Solidity Basics: Familiarize yourself with Solidity's syntax, data types, functions, and object-oriented concepts. Understand how to write, deploy, and interact with smart contracts.

> Smart Contract Development: Practice building smart contracts, handling events, managing data storage, and implementing security measures to prevent vulnerabilities like reentrancy attacks or integer overflow.

3. Blockchain Security Best Practices:

Smart Contract Auditing: Learn to audit and review smart contracts to identify and fix potential vulnerabilities.

Encryption and Hashing: Understand cryptographic principles, hashing algorithms, and encryption methods to ensure secure data storage and transmission.

Security Standards: Familiarize yourself with security standards and best practices specific to blockchain, such as OWASP Top 10 for Blockchain.

4. Networking and Community Engagement:

Online Communities: Engage in blockchain-related forums, social media groups, and platforms like GitHub. Contribute to projects, share knowledge, and learn from others in the community.

Meetups and Events: Attend blockchain-related meetups, conferences, workshops, and hackathons. Networking helps in learning from industry experts and building connections.

5. Continuous Learning and Adaptability:

Stay Updated: Blockchain technology evolves rapidly. Follow industry news, research papers, and updates on new protocols, consensus mechanisms, and trends.

Adaptability: Be ready to learn new tools, frameworks, and emerging technologies in the blockchain space. Adaptability is key to staying relevant and competitive.

Building a career in blockchain requires a blend of technical expertise, security awareness, continuous learning, and active engagement within the blockchain community. Mastering programming languages, understanding smart contract development, emphasizing security practices, networking, and staying adaptable are essential steps toward a successful blockchain career.

Chapter 5: Getting Started in Blockchain Careers

Here's a comprehensive guide to getting started in blockchain careers:

1. Education and Certifications:

> Blockchain Courses and Degrees: Consider enrolling in online courses, bootcamps, or university programs specializing in blockchain technology. Look for courses covering blockchain fundamentals, smart contract development, and decentralized applications.

> Certifications: Pursue certifications from reputable organizations like Certified Blockchain Developer (CBD), The Blockchain Council, Ethereum Developer, or certifications from platforms like Coursera, Udacity, or ConsenSys Academy.

2. Building a Strong Portfolio:

> Hands-On Projects: Develop projects showcasing your blockchain skills. Create smart contracts, DApps, or contribute to open-source blockchain projects on platforms like GitHub.

> Case Studies and Research: Write blog posts, articles, or case studies about blockchain trends, industry applications, or technical tutorials. A strong portfolio demonstrates practical knowledge and expertise.

3. Networking and Community Engagement:

Online Communities: Join blockchain-related forums, subreddits, and platforms like Stack Overflow, Reddit's r/ethereum or r/bitcoin, and specialized blockchain forums to engage with the community and seek advice.

Meetups and Events: Attend local or virtual blockchain meetups, conferences, and workshops. Networking with professionals in the field can open up opportunities and provide valuable insights.

4. Job Search Strategies in the Blockchain Industry:

Specialized Job Boards: Explore job listings on specialized blockchain job boards like Crypto Jobs List, AngelList, or ConsenSys Jobs, as well as mainstream job platforms that feature blockchain positions.

Tailored Resumes and Cover Letters: Customize your resume and cover letter to highlight relevant blockchain skills and experiences for each job application.

LinkedIn and Professional Profiles: Optimize your LinkedIn profile to showcase your blockchain expertise, projects, certifications, and connect with professionals in the industry.

5. Freelancing and Remote Opportunities:

Freelance Platforms: Explore freelance platforms like Upwork, Freelancer, or Toptal, which occasionally feature blockchain-related projects. Highlight your skills and previous blockchain projects in your profile.

Remote Job Opportunities: Many blockchain companies offer remote positions. Look for remote job postings on company websites, job boards, or remote work platforms specifically catering to tech roles.

Starting a career in blockchain involves a mix of education, practical experience, networking, and strategic job searching. Building a strong educational foundation, showcasing practical skills through projects, networking within the blockchain community, and exploring various job search avenues can significantly enhance your prospects in the blockchain industry.

Thank You For Your Purchase!

Dear Reader,

If you have enjoyed the content of this book and have learned something new, I've accomplished my task. I ask of you just a small favor. *Please leave a book review rating on the website of purchase/download, refer this book to a friend, and post about this book and others, listed below, on social media.*

For a deeper dive into the intricacies of Blockchain Technology and Cryptocurrency, consider checking out one of my other books, listed below.

All books listed are available on all major online bookstore retailers such as Amazon, Google Play Books, Apple Books, Barnes and Noble, etc.

I am very passionate about cryptocurrency and blockchain technology. My goal is to educate the masses about this amazing technology. Please assist in promoting my books online. My goal is 1M downloads.

THANK YOU in advance for supporting my projects.

Sincerely,

Michael McNaught.

Contact: thecryptocurrencylibrary@gmail.com

List of my other books:

1. Bitcoin: King of the Coins

2. Cryptocurrency Chronicles: Unlocking The Secrets Of Blockchain Technology

3. A Deep Dive Into The Top 50 Cryptocurrencies: A DYOR (Do Your Own Research) Guide

4. Common Crypto Investment Pitfalls and How To Avoid: A DYOR (Do Your Own Research) Guide

5. The Comprehensive Blockchain Technology Career Guide: Decentralizing Your Potential

6. A Practical Guide To Saving in Cryptocurrency: An Alternative To The Traditional System

7. An Introduction To Cryptocurrency Laws in the United States: A Simplified And Concise Guide

8. The Digital Revolution: Central Bank Digital Currencies (CBDC) Unveiled

9. Web 3.0: Unleashing The Power Of Decentralized Connectivity

10. Decentralized Finance (DeFi): Unlocking The Future of Financial Freedom

11. Artificial Intelligence (AI) Unleashed: Exploring The Boundless Potential of AI

Two (2) **FREE** ebook downloads:
https://www.free-ebooks.net/search/michael+mcnaught#gs.17gmqo

Please leave a book review rating on the website of purchase/download!

www.ingramcontent.com/pod-product-compliance
Lightning Source LLC
LaVergne TN
LVHW051752050326
832903LV00029B/2865